Imagining Liam

David Scott

Imagining Liam is an original play written by David Scott, first performed by Company D Theatre. Copyright 2017. All rights reserved. Reproduction and performance of Imagining Liam without permission of the author is forbidden except in the case of short excerpts for educational purposes. For permission to perform this play, contact the author by

Email: davidarts@eircom.net.
Phone: +353 87 759 6715
www.davidscott.ie

Imagining Liam
by
David Scott

Copyright 2017

Dramatis Personae

Robert Leversedge, 30, a largish man
Steve Cartmell, 35, more slight than Robert
Maggie Ramsay, late 20's or early 30's
Barman
Guard
Barman and Guard may be played by the same actor

Imagining Liam

ACT I

Scene 1

Robert Leversedge stands centre-stage. He has a pint of beer in his hand. It's half- drunk.

Voices. These can be real or recorded. It's clearly Robert's birthday. He is thirty.

Voices: (a combination of) Happy Birthday mate! Big three-oh! You're an old man now! When are you going to put a ring on Janice? No more messing around! Have a pint. It's my round. What are ya drinking? You need to ask for a raise, working that joint day in and...

Robert: No lads, I can't I have to drive.

Another pint is brought out to him. It arrives into his hand from a Barman.

Barman: From those lads across the bar there. For your birthday.

Robert: Ah shit. I have to drive. Ok. Thanks! *(He signals to the "lads across the bar")* Cheers!

Robert finishes the half full pint and sips the new one.

Robert: Seriously lads, that's all then. I gotta drive. I can't leave the car there. It'll get clamped.

Voices: Let em clamp it. We'll pay to get it out.

Robert: No way! I have to work in the morning. I'll need it.

Voice: *(Laughter)* Call in sick. Fucking shit hole you work in there anyway.

Robert: Ha ha! Nope. I'm off after this one.

(Another pint arrives from the Barman. He takes the empty glass from his hand and puts a full one in it. Now Robert has two practically full pints, one in each hand.)

Robert: That'll do! Jesus H Chris…

SLAM!

With a sudden sound and lighting change, the prison cell is revealed behind him. Two bunk beds. A toilet. A sink. A small locker at the foot of each bunk. Perhaps a couple of small tables and chairs. It's rudimentary, but enough to facilitate the action of the play.

A costume change on stage reveals Robert's prison track pants and T-shirt or grey sweater. A blanket, soap and towel are thrust into his hands by a Guard.

Steven sits on one of the beds. The other prisoner, Steve Cartmell, is a middle-thirties bloke. Neat. He has been there for some time. He has made his half of the cell his home including some nick-knacks, books, writing equipment and a statue of the Virgin Mary.

Scene 2

Guard: Leversedge, this is your home. Look after it.

Now. You're not a violent man. You made a stupid mistake didn't you Leversedge?

Robert: If you say so.

Guard: Don't give me lip. You give me problems I'll make your life a living hell.

Robert: It already is.

Guard: Man, you have no idea.

Up the corridor is a nest of vermin you can't even imagine. Murderers, gangsters, rapists and drug lords. Stay away. Do you hear me?

Robert: Yes Guard.

Guard: You stay away from them and they'll stay away from you. This is your cellmate, also a non-violent offender as far as we know. Isn't that right Cartmell?

Steve: Clean as a whistle Guard.

Guard: Keep your noses clean and everything will be just fine. Don't give me any reason to go heavy and I go light. Got it?

Robert: Got it.

Guard: You know the routine. Any questions, ask him. If he doesn't know, work it out yourself. Enjoy.

(The Guard exits. Robert steps back towards his bed.)

Steve: You must be Robert.

(Robert doesn't answer.)

Steve: All right, buddy. Suit yourself.

(No answer. Robert sorts out his stuff. Makes his bed, lays his towel and soap down. He sits on the bed. Pause.)

Steve: You'll have to talk eventually. Unless you're only in for a day or two. Which you're not. I can tell.

(Silence.)

Steve: Did you bring any treats? Biscuits?

(Pause.)

Steve: Anything?

(Silence. Robert stares ahead.)

Steve: There were sausages at breakfast this morning. Tasted like cardboard. But better than porridge.
   (Pause.) Don't mind him about all the vermin up the way. They're too busy dealing with eachother. Guard's just trying to spook you. Besides, you look big enough to take care of yourself.
   (Pause.) Look, I know it's a shock to the system. I went through it myself. Obviously.

(Silence.)

Steve: Okay. Well, I'm just writing here. I'll let you settle. When you're ready to talk, you know where to find me.
   I won't be... far away.

(Pause.)

Robert: That the only toilet?

Steve: Yep.

Robert: How do we… use it?

Steve: You want a lesson in how to use a toilet?

Robert: You know what I mean.

Steve: Not really.

Robert: If I need to go, what do you do?

Steve: I close my eyes and think of Ireland.

Robert: I'm not joking. I can't piss in front of you.

Steve: You piss in front of lads all the time at urinals in bars. You've been doing it for years. Why so shy?

Robert: Maybe. But I don't shit in front of people.

Steve: It's not that big a deal. You get used to it.

Robert: Doesn't it stink in here? After a shit?

Steve: Yes.

(Pause.)

Steve: Okay. Look. The last lad who had that bunk, we just worked out a system. He always needed to go at 11:30am or thereabouts. That's yard time. So I'd go out to the yard while he did his business. Yea?

Robert: What was your time?

Steve: Just after dinner. About 5pm. He stayed in the mess. I came back here and took a shit. Now there were the odd emergency situations. You just deal with it.

Robert: I usually go at 5pm too.

Steve: Then someone has to change his clock.

(Pause.)

Robert: Fuck.

Steve: It's not so bad. They show most of the big matches. There's movies. You know. It's not so bad.

Robert: What's the point?

Steve: Correction and rehabilitation my friend.

Robert: Sitting around watching matches and movies and getting fed.

Steve: Correction and rehabilitation my friend.

Robert: Shit.

(Pause.)

Robert: Shit. I don't think I can hack this.

Steve: You'll be all right. I know what you're going through. Just breathe. If you need to punch something, make it not me.

Robert: Oh my god.

Steve: Don't use the lord's name please.

(Pause.)

Robert: Are you fucking kidding me?

Steve: No. It's my one thing. I'm not demanding. I'm asking. I'm not a fighting man. I'm a business man. I can't "take you out" and get all macho with you. You could snap my neck like a chicken I'm sure. I'm not demanding. I'm just asking.

Robert: Jesus Christ.

Steve: Thanks for your generosity Robert.

Robert: I have a thing too.

Steve: What's your thing.

Robert: Anal sex.

Steve: Fine.

Robert: I won't use your god's name in vain. You provide your arse for anal sex.

Steve: Deal.

(Pause.)

Robert: I don't want anal sex.

Steve: I didn't think so. You've never been in prison before have you?

Robert: Is that all a myth? Butt fucking and all?

Steve: It's not a myth. But it's not a gay sauna either.

Robert: Good. The fewer faggots I have to beat to a fucking pulp in here, the better.

(Pause.)

Robert: What's your name?

Steve: Steve.

(Pause.)

Robert: Robert.

Steve: I know.

(Pause.)

Robert: How long are you in here?

Steve: Two years. Five to go.

Robert: Fucking hell! What did you do?

Steve: I don't like to talk about it.

(Pause.)

Steve: You?

Robert: I don't like to/ talk about it.

Steve: /talk about it. I get ya. How long?

Robert: Four years.

Steve: Four years? That all?

Robert: What do you mean?

Steve: Never mind.

Robert: Do you know what I did?

Steve: No. It's just I got seven and you got four. I wasn't making any other point…

Robert: Bullshit. You knew my name. You watch the news in here with your matches and movies Steve?

Steve: Yes we do.

Robert: Then you know what I did.

Steve: I do.

(Pause.)

Robert: Say it.

Steve: No.

Robert: Go on. I want to hear how you word it.

Steve: It's not my business, Robert. I'm not getting involved.

Robert: No no no. If we're going to live in this little room together for four years, you better speak up. We have to know where we stand, Steve.

Steve: Robert, I have no opinion…

Robert: Your opinion lies in your phrasing of my crime. Speak up, Steve. Or maybe I will snap your neck like a chicken.

Steve: I'm not saying anything.

(Robert stands and steps towards Steve who sits calmly on the side of his bed.)

Steve: All right. I don't need my head kicked in today.

Robert: Speak up.

(Pause.)

Steve: You killed a kid.

(Pause.)

Robert: Now that's where you're wrong, Steve. This is where we need to get something straight. A kid ran out in front of my car. Say it.

Steve: A kid ran out in front of your car.

Robert: That's it. That's my crime. You understand me?

Steve: Four years. Sounds like the kid should have got four years since it's all his fault, Robert.

Robert: The kid got life. Or Death. Whichever way you want to put it.

(Pause. Robert sits back down on his bed.)

Steve: All right, Robert. Let's not talk about it anymore.

Robert: Let's not.

(Pause.)

Robert: You seem like you've made yourself at home.

Steve: Might as well. Got nowhere else to go.

Robert: *(Seeing his papers and stationary.)* You write?

Steve: Sometimes.

Robert: What do you write? Letters to your sweetheart?

Steve: Something like that.

(Pause.)

16

Robert: This is fucking horrible.

Steve: It's not so bad. There's a routine. You get up, you eat, you have some open door time. You know. You get to wander around a bit. There's a communal area. A yard for when it's not pissing with rain. A TV. Mostly the others watch premier league. You like premier league?

Robert: It's ok.

Steve: Who do you support?

Robert: Liverpool for my sins. My old man was from there. We travelled a lot with his work. But he's from there originally. My mother's from here. But she hates this country. You?

Steve: I don't. I just watch it because there's no choice. Or I read.

Robert: What do you read?

Steve: Whatever. There's a library. Mostly literature. I didn't get to go to college. Parents didn't have the dough and then died leaving nothing much. So I read the stuff I missed out on really. Shakespeare. Wilde. Shaw. Racine. And psychology too. Jung. Stuff like that.

Robert: You'll have a degree by the time you get out of here.

Steve: Two degrees.

(Pause.)

Robert: Is it violent?

Steve: Violent?

Robert: Yeah. You know. In here.

Steve: Sure. It can be. But you can avoid it. There's a lot of drugs. Most of the fights are about that.

Robert: You ever been stabbed or…

Steve: Anal sex?

Robert: … anything?

Steve: Nah. There's nothing they want from me. I got beaten up a couple of times. Nothing too bad.

(Pause.)

Robert: Fucking hell.

(Pause.)

Steve: Look. It's really not all that bad. It's the boredom that gets you the most. Every day's the same. But you're warm and you're fed.

Robert: Brilliant.

Steve: What did you do for a living?

Robert: Accountant.

Steve: Yawn.

Robert: Why does everybody do that? Why is accountancy the universal symbol for boredom? It's a job. I make sure people's tax returns are right for them. What the fuck?

Steve: Sorry. Family?

Robert: No.

Steve: Girl?

18

Robert: No.

Steve: Anyone who'll visit you?

Robert: No. A few mates. My parents are alive but they live in England. They might drop by. They came over for the trial but it wore them out. They've gone back. I have a sister. She hates me. And she lives in San Fran.
     You?

Steve: Nah. I'm a lone wolf.

Robert: Must be someone.

Steve: Not really.

(Pause.)

Robert: How do you… get used to this?

Steve: I don't know. But it happens.
     If you have visitors get them to bring treats.

Roberts: Treats? What are you, a child?

Steve: We're all children.

(Robert looks at him. Fade.)

Scene 3

Night.
Steve is lying on his bed. He sleeps.
Robert is sitting on his bed, also asleep. He dreams.
Maggie enters.

Robert: Hello.

Maggie: Hello. Did they tell you I was coming to see you?

Robert: No. But I knew you would sooner or later. What do you want? Didn't you say all you wanted to say in the court? All the screaming and crying and victim impact carry-on?

Maggie: I came because it's not over. He's not dead.

Robert: Trust me. He's dead. I saw him.

Maggie: Not to me he's not.

Robert: I can't do anything about that. I can't turn back the clock. Neither can you.

Maggie: I know that. But I need to talk to you. I need to always be talking to you. I talk to you in my mind. I think about you every day. You're the man who took my boy away.

Robert: I didn't take him away from you, Maggie. You left your gate open and he ran out. If it wasn't me driving up that road it would have been someone else. You know it and I know it. Even the Judge knew it. But he had to come down hard because it's the popular thing to do.

Maggie: You'd been drinking.

Robert: I had three pints for my birthday.

Maggie: It doesn't matter.

Robert: Would you stop repeating the TV, Maggie. You know as well as I do a few pints makes no difference at all to driving a fucking car. I can walk a fucking tightrope between two skyscrapers after three pints. Every man can. Your kid ran out in front of my car and I hit the brakes in the same time a Pioneer would have.

I was coming up to the rise. There's a dip there. Just at the top of the rise. I wasn't speeding. It was bright still. The light was good, the road was dry. I saw your black gate from way back, half-way up the rise. It was open. I noticed it was open, thought nothing of it and kept going. I knew there was a dip at the top of that rise so I slowed down. I slowed down even more because I knew I'd get butterflies going over that rise at any kind of pace. I hate butterflies. I hate that feeling in the belly when you lift over a rise and down into a dip. So I slowed down even more.

Look I said all this in court. Why do you want to hear it again? He came shooting out like a maniac. I saw him plain as day. Green jeans, red shoes, blue shirt. Little red cap. I hit those brakes so hard I thought my foot was going to go through the floor. But it was just too late. He gave me no chance, Maggie.

Maggie: His little back broke and he hit his head on the road and broke his skull.

Robert: Please. I know. I know that's what happened. I know that. I saw him.

Maggie: How can you forgive yourself?

Robert: Maggie! There's nothing to forgive. It wasn't my fault!

Maggie: It was my fault.

Robert: No Maggie. It's nobody's fault. He was six years old. He was a kid and he was fast on his feet. These things happen Maggie. Accidents happen. But the fact that I drank three pints that lunch time isn't going to help you. Being able to make me out to be a villain isn't going to make it any easier for you to move on. I'm going to have to stay in this fucking place for four years because of those three pints. If you don't think that's punishment enough, I don't know what else to say to you.

Maggie: I want you to take responsibility. Why couldn't you say you were sorry?

Robert: Because I didn't do anything wrong! Any other driver on this planet would have hit Liam that day. I said I was sorry for your loss. And I am. Of course I am. I'm genuinely heartbroken for you. But if I'd apologized for killing him, which is what the Judge and everyone else wanted me to do, I would have basically admitted to manslaughter. How can I admit to manslaughter when it was an accident? The Judge would have given me ten years instead of four.

(Steve is still in his bed. But his eyes are open and he is clearly listening.)

Maggie: Liam played guitar. Did you know that?

Robert: No.

Maggie: He was really good. For his age I mean. He was a bit of a prodigy his teacher said.

Robert: That's nice.

Maggie: You know what he wanted the most in the world?

Robert: What's that?

Maggie: To play his guitar on the Late Late Toy Show. Can you believe that? We were going to apply for this Christmas.

Robert: I'm sure he would have got picked.

Maggie: I'm sure too.
He had this favourite piece. It was called The River. It sounded like a river when he played it. He wrote it. Can you believe that? A six year old writing his own tunes. He was really good at it.

Robert: That's lovely Maggie.

Maggie: He had lots of toys too you know. Soft toys. All kinds of fluffy friends. He collected them.

Robert: I know, Maggie.

Maggie: He said they kept him safe in his bed at night. They minded him.

(Pause.)

Maggie: I'm going to go now.

Robert: Okay.

Maggie: I want you to be sorry.

Robert: I can't Maggie. I can't say that. It's not right to say it.

(Maggie turns to go.)

Robert: Maggie.

(She turns back.)

Robert: You can visit any time you want to. I'm not a bad person. I want to help you to grieve. I really do. Come anytime.

(Maggie exits.)

Scene 4

Morning. Natural light fills the cell.
Steve is already up and dressed. He goes through a set of exercises as he speaks. The exercises are awkward.
Robert stirs.

Steve: Good morning sunshine.

Robert: Why so bright?

Steve: You've been here a week and this is the first sunny day there's been. It really lights up in here when the sun fills it.

Robert: What are you doing?

Steve: Exercising.

Robert: You exercise once a week?

Steve: Yes I do. Whether I need it or not.

Robert: You're probably not achieving much doing it once a week.

Steve: I know. But it's better than what you've been doing for your first week. Eating shitting and sleeping. You better find other stuff to do, Rob.

Robert: Let me worry about me, Steve.

Steve: Got to get the blood pumping Steve. Otherwise you'll rot. Exercising's good. For the mind too. Really, I do it when I can't sleep.

Robert: Do you have trouble sleeping?

Steve: I do while you're jabbering away over there half the night.

Robert: Have I been talking in my sleep?

Steve: Like a broadcaster.

Robert: I've been known to do that.

Steve: Known by whom? Do you have a girl waiting for you on the outside, prisoner?

Robert: I did. But she dumped me during the trial. *(Mimicking her.)* "It's all too much for me!" It was too much for your reputation amongst your mates.

Steve: All women are bitches.

Robert: Amen.

Steve: *(Picking up his statue)* Except the Virgin Mary.

Robert: Amen.

Steve: Are you a believer, Robert?

Robert: Absolutely fucking not.

Steve: An atheist?

Robert: Yes. I can't abide Christianity. Or fucking Islam or fucking any of it. Bunch of arseholes raping kids and stoning women and blowing eachother up. It's not God I have a problem with. It's religious cunts.

Steve: Are you about to blaspheme, Robert.

Robert: Probably.

Steve: Go on. I give thee leave to blaspheme.

Robert: I'll just offend you.

Steve: Go on. Offend me. It'll give me something to struggle with. Alleviate the boredom.

Robert: Very well. You were warned. So you attest to a religion whose main symbol is an innocent man nailed to a cross.

Steve: And?

Robert: Think about that. He's nailed to a cross. Nailed through his hands and feet, with a crown of thorns jammed onto his head. This is the symbol that Christian people have to look at from the moment they're born, all their lives. The entire crucifixion is this process of extreme torture and violence. As such, those people exposed to that extreme violence and torture, AS CHILDREN let's remember, are desensitized to violence and torture from a very early age.

As a result, you have a religion whose center is extreme violence and torture and then you find out that the clergy of those Christian orders seem to be able to commit acts of extreme violence and torture on the most vulnerable children in their care.

When a new revelation hits the airwaves of raped children or buried babies, everyone is so flabbergasted! I'm not. I'm not surprised at all that people completely desensitised to pain and torture can inflict it upon tiny children and feel no shame or remorse at all. It makes perfect fucking sense to me.

They're all fucking psychopaths.

Steve: You do operate in absolutes, my friend.

Robert: I operate from conviction and outrage, Steve. Take your Virgin Mary there.

Steve: Go easy.

Robert: Apart from a hooker, she's really the only woman in the whole Christian story and she's a virgin. You talk about absolutes? The only two women in the story are a prostitute who requires forgiveness from a man, and a Virgin who is valid because she's had no sex at all. What the fuck does that say to young Christian women?

How are they supposed to figure out themselves in a sexual sense when women are represented like that in their core religious indoctrination? Imagine being a little girl being brought up under that shit?

Steve: It teaches that purity is the goal. Purity is simplest and most perfect.

Robert: But nobody is pure. Where's the book that teaches you how to be a human being? Where's the book that teaches women how to be real, human women with sexual desires and needs and a fucking brain that goes beyond that. Your Virgin Mary didn't achieve anything. She stood by, powerless, while the Romans tortured her son to death at the behest of another bunch of animal- sacrificing psychos, the Jews. Don't you get that? The only two women in the book are tools. One vilified for her sexuality and the other rendered impotent in every sense.

And why does having sex have to be synonymous with impurity anyway? What business did Christianity have making us all believe that the very act that creates life and affirms love is dirty? Why is one of the few things that feels good in this shitty world criminalized by your religion, Steve?

Your religion is fucked in the head. Blasphemy over.

Steve: Robert, I take your point.

(Pause.)

Robert: You do?

Steve: Yes, I do.

I suppose that to me, the Virgin is uncomplicated. She's calm. She's untouched. Don't you ever want that? To be calm? To be untouched?

Robert: You mean a virgin?

Steve: Not sexually.

(Pause.)

Robert: Okay. I see where you're going. Are you asking me if I would prefer my crime to be lifted from me? Are you asking if I want the purity I felt before what happened back in my life?

Steve: Maybe I am.

Robert: If I could magic away what happened to that little boy, I would. Of course I would. Has my life changed since that happened? Yes. Of course it has. Look at me. Rotting away in here with you. Life's a little different. No job, no girlfriend, no freedom.

Steve: Much simpler.

Robert: Sure.

Steve: And if you could take it away. Take away that moment of change that happened in your life. Would you?

Robert: Yes.

Steve: Don't you like this simplicity?

Robert: No. I hate it.

Steve: So you'd like to turn back the clock and rewrite time? Rewrite it so it's untouched by this moment of... whatever you call it... crime, mistake, accident.

Robert: Accident. Yes, of course.

Steve: That's forgiveness.

(Pause.)

Steve: That's what Christ is all about. Forget about God. I don't care if you believe in God or not. Frankly, I don't either. But I believe in forgiveness. I believe in that. I hang onto it.

But Robert, to have it, you have to earn it. You have to be honest, not with God, or Christ or anyone else. You have to be honest with yourself. Only you can set yourself free.

Robert: I am free.

Steve: I don't think so.

Robert: In my own mind I am. In my conscience I am.

Steve: You seem very concerned about the welfare of children.

Robert: What? Because I don't think they should be raped and buried in septic tanks?

Steve: Because you know that the ideal world is a world for children.

Robert: That's probably true. A world that's pure and fun and playful. Sure why not?

Steve: A world where a kid could run out his own front gate and not get killed?

Robert: Are you trying to equate what I did to what the clergy did to kids?

Steve: Of course not. But man, you drank alcohol and drove up a residential street.

(Robert stands and advances on Steve.)

Robert: Watch your step. I don't need your judgment. I've had all the fucking judgment I can stomach. I don't need to justify myself to you. Back off.

Steve: Easy, champ.
  What I'm saying is, your life has been simplified by what happened. Yet you don't want that simplicity, yet you want a simple

world made for children, because we're all children, pure and simple. We just want to live and be happy. Do you want simplicity or not?

Robert: I'm lost. You've lost me.

(The Guard enters with a guitar in a guitar case and a small child's toy. A teddy bear or some such. The guitar is small. Child-sized.)

Guard: Everything all right here boys?

Steve: All good in the hood, Guard.

Guard: The fucking hood.
     Leversedge, You have a delivery.

Robert: A guitar?

Guard: Now, listen up. It's from the woman whose kid you killed. This is really important, so listen up. You don't have to receive anything from her. This was passed by the Judge himself. It's allowed under rare circumstances. But you're not under any obligation to receive it. Frankly I'd prefer if you didn't because I bet you're shit at it and I'll have to listen to you beating on the thing for four years.
     And there's rules.
     There's some nasty strings on this thing. You can have it for an hour and a half each day during open time. That means the cell door stays open. It means Cartmell here has to be in the cell with you constantly during that hour and a half.
     At the end of the hour and a half it's returned to the Guard on duty and locked away. It'll be checked each time to make sure there's still six fucking strings on it. Got it?

Robert: I got it.

Guard: If there was a notion that you or him might be a suicide risk, you wouldn't have this. If the psychologist or anyone else gets a whiff you might be thinking of topping yourself, no more guitar.

Leversedge, would you like to accept these deliveries on those terms?

Robert: Sure. Why not?

Guard: *(Referring to the soft toy.)* And… this.

Robert: Sure.

(The Guard tosses it to Robert.)

Guard: Can you play the guitar Leversedge?

Robert: Not really.

Guard: Fucking lovely. What a treat for the rest of us. Right. I'll drop it to you at open time. Have a nice morning, ladies.

Steve: See you, John.

Guard: Guard to you, Cartmell.

Steve: *(Saluting)* Yes Guard.

(Exit Guard.)

Steve: This may effect our toileting routine.
    What was that?

Robert: It's the kid's guitar.

Steve: It looks child sized all right.

Robert: It was one of the things the mother brought up in the court. Said he was learning the guitar. Wanted to play it on the Late Late Toy Show.

(Pause.)

Steve: That's rough.

Robert: Yeah. Well when she visited I said I'd do anything she wanted to help her... you know... grieve. I guess this is what she wanted.

Steve: Visited. She visited you while you were in custody during the trial? That's unorthodox.

Robert: No. Yesterday evening.

Steve: I didn't know she visited you yesterday.

Robert: Last night. You were sleeping right there on that bed. You obviously didn't have any insomnia last night.

(Pause.)

Steve: Robert, no one was in here last night except you and me.

Robert: And Maggie. She was here for about ten minutes.

Steve: No mate. She wasn't.

Robert: You were asleep. You were right there the whole time.

Steve: Robert, there's no way a visitor would be allowed into this cell. Not even the psychiatrists or psych staff are allowed. Maybe a doctor if you're so sick you can't get out of bed, in which case you'd be transferred to the infirmary.

Robert: What are you talking about? She was right here.

Steve: No. Visitors see you in the visiting hall or in a private room. And they see you during visiting hours which is on a Sunday afternoon.

(Pause. Robert is silent and very still.)

Steve: Rob, you were talking in your sleep. You were talking a lot. You said Maggie. That's her name, right? But the rest was gibberish. I couldn't make it out.

(Pause.)

Robert: Fucking hell. Must have been a dream. It was so real.

(Pause.)

Steve: Do you want to see the shrink? You can just request one. It's not a big deal.

Robert: No.

Steve: It's okay. It happens. Especially in the first few weeks. Your whole environment is screwed around. You can have some weird dreams. Very lucid. They just give you some meds to help you keep calm and sleep.

Robert: *(Shaken.)* Okay.
   I'm going to get some breakfast.

Scene 5

Steve is asleep.

Maggie enters. Robert sits on the side of his bed, "asleep" and looks at her for some time.

Robert: I know you're not real.

Maggie: Did you get my presents?

Robert: Yes.

Maggie: Did you play it?

Robert: No. I just looked at it.

Maggie: Why didn't you play it?

Robert: I don't know how.

Maggie: That's not it.

Robert: It didn't seem right. *(Pause.)* I was imagining his little hands on it. Playing it. It didn't seem right to play it.

Maggie: I want you to play it.

Robert: I don't have to do what you want, Maggie.

(Steve wakes and slowly stands.)

Maggie: I need you to play it.

Robert: Why?

Maggie: Because I need to hear it. The house is so quiet. It used to be filled with his sounds. My favourite was his guitar. Play it. Please play it.

Robert: Maggie, you won't hear it in your house from here. I can't play it for you. If I play it, it'll be heard by a bunch of convicts and guards in this hole that I have to spend the next four years of my life in.

Maggie: Find a way. Please.
    I'm so alone. My heart. There's an empty tin can here. Here in my chest. It's hollow. I'm dying inside. I need you to play it. I need you to be sorry.

Robert: Please Maggie. Please leave me be.

(Exit Maggie. Steve is standing.)

Steve: Wake up Rob.

(Robert stays motionless, sitting on the side of the bed. In a moment or two he comes too.)

Robert: What?

Steve: You were asleep.

Robert: I know I was asleep, shithead, why did you wake me?

Steve: You're sitting on the side of your bed sound asleep talking to the air.

(Pause. He realizes.)

Robert: Did you see her?

Steve: No mate.

Robert: Ok. Sorry. Go back to sleep.

Steve: It's ok. I think I'll write for a while.

Robert: What is all that writing?

Steve: It's nothing much. Musings. And letters.

Robert: Are you writing a memoir?

Steve: Kind of.

Robert: Who are the letters too?

Steve: The President.

Robert: Ah. Asking for a more lenient sentence?

Steve: Not quite. In a way, yes.

Robert: Good luck with that. They'll be in a bin in the Phoenix Park.

Steve: I doubt they even leave here. But they keep me busy.

Robert: Then why bother?

Steve: I send some to other places. Newspapers. My boyfriend.

(Pause.)

Robert: Your boyfriend?

Steve: Yes. Well. He's married to a woman, but we have a thing. It's not exactly an official thing.

Robert: I didn't know you were gay.

Steve: No. I figured you didn't.

Robert: That anal sex thing. I was… that was…

Steve: Yes, what was that exactly?

Robert: Now look, don't get the wrong idea. I was being…

Steve: Ironical? Insensitive? Offensive?

Robert: I…

Steve: It's fine. I like being threatened with my own sexual preferences. And I'm glad you haven't had to beat up any faggots since you've been here.

Robert: No, I'm…

Steve: Homophobic?

Robert: Sorry. And fuck no, I'm not homophobic.

Steve: Really? Then you won't mind giving me some anal sex then. It's been a long time.

Robert: Steve. I'm sorry. I was making an entirely different point. It was my first day in here. I was shaken up.

Steve: It's fine.

Robert: No, it's not fine. I was an ass.

Steve: It's all right.

Robert: No. You deserve better than that. I'm really sorry. Genuinely.

(Pause.)

Steve: Apology accepted.

(Pause.)

Robert: Thank you.

(Pause.)

Robert: What's his name?

Steve: John.

Robert: John. Is he a nice guy?

Steve: He's a little bewildered.

Robert: Sounds like it. Any kids?

Steve: He has a daughter. Teenager. They're having a lot of trouble with her. She's a bit messed up.

Robert: He writes to you too?

Steve: Sure. Every couple of weeks. Sometimes more.

Robert: What's wrong with the daughter?

Steve: Long, long story.

Robert: What's the nub?

Steve: The nub is she was raped by her uncle when she was eleven.

(Pause.)

Robert: Fuck.

Steve: He was a priest.

Robert: Fuck. Did they get him?

Steve: He served two and a half years. He's out now. No one's exactly sure where he is. America John reckons.

Robert: That's a fucking appalling sentence for rape.

Steve: I know. But she was consenting and highly sexed for her age. That's what the solicitors kept drumming into the Judge's head. Plus, he's a priest. Anyone else would have got nine years.

(Pause.)

Robert: You're a complex man, Steve.

Steve: That's an odd thing to say.

Robert: You are. You have your statue of the Virgin there. You defend the Church. You're gay in a religion that utterly hates your type. Yet you keep faith. You're a walking contradiction.

Steve: I guess.

Robert: Man, if I was a member of an organization and I found out it was basically the world's biggest pedophile ring, I'd leave that organization. I'd rescind my membership. But you just truck on. The world never ceases to confuse me.

Steve: I'm a walking contradiction. What song was that?

Robert: Green Day.

Steve: No, there's an older one. Partly truth, partly fiction… That one.

Robert: Don't know.

Steve: It'll come to me.

Robert: You didn't answer my question.

Steve: What was the question?

Robert: How do you reconcile it?

Steve: I already told you. Forgiveness.

Robert: But how do you do that? How do you forgive a prick that takes advantage of an eleven year old girl? Here's a case in point. You're gay. Your people were vilified for centuries. You were blasted with fire hoses and beaten up and tortured in prison cells. Still this shit is government sanctioned in countries all over the world and your religion supports those views. How do you forgive that?

Steve: Is there any point in not forgiving it?

Robert: YES! The point is you don't tolerate it. You stand up and fight it.

Steve: You're mistaking forgiveness for tolerance. I don't tolerate anything. But I do forgive. I took you to task over the way you behaved on your first day here. Didn't I?

Robert: Yes.

Steve: And I forgave you. I still don't think you were right. I'm not tolerating what you did and said and I won't tolerate it again. But you were genuinely sorry. And I forgave you. And now we're moving on. Right?

Robert: But this fucking priest... he got two and a half years.

Steve: That's true. And that's intolerable. And I am writing many letters to the highest office in the land about it because justice in this country is sick and needs to be fixed.

Robert: But you forgive this priest?

Steve: No.

Robert: You don't forgive him? You wreck my head, man, seriously.

Steve: No. Because he was not genuinely sorry. He never apologized to me. He never apologized to her. He never apologized to John. He made all the excuses under the sun. She came onto him. He was sexually frustrated because he was a priest to the point of being mentally ill. Yada yada yada. There's no remorse in him. And wherever he is now he's probably doing the same thing. As far as we know, he wasn't even removed from the priesthood. The fact is, it doesn't matter what his excuses are. At the moment of the crunch, he raped that little girl. It was a terrible moment of weakness. And whether she thought she wanted that or not, he made an awful mistake and exploited a little girl who's sexual development, and frankly her life, has now been ruined beyond all recognition. That's what he did. And if he could simply admit to that, excuses or not, and ask for the forgiveness of that little girl and her parents and the society around him that he has so debased and offended by doing that, then I would forgive him, yes. And I would also expect him to get the time he deserves for it too, which he didn't.

I don't forgive someone who isn't sorry. You were sorry. And I don't believe you will use my sexuality as a threat anymore. You said things you regret in a moment of weakness. You apologized and you are forgiven. He is not.

(A long pause.)

Robert: I didn't kill that little boy.

Steve: Fine, Robert. You didn't. So what did you do?

Robert: I drank three pints and drove a car.

Steve: Good for you. If that's what your conscience tells you, good for you. I think the voices in your head are telling you something else.

I don't think I'm going to write after all. Goodnight.

(The lights fade as Steve lies down.)

Scene 6

Day
There are several soft toys now in the cell now, lined up on Robert's bed.
Steve writes.
Robert slowly takes the guitar out of its case. He looks at it and lays it on the bed.
He then opens a pocket in the case and takes out some sheet music.

Steve: How many of his toys is she going to send you?

Robert: I don't know. If it helps her, I don't mind taking them.

Steve: What's that?

Robert: It's a piece of music. It's called The River. It was his favourite piece apparently. He wanted to play it on the Late Late Toy Show at Christmas.

Steve: Play it.

Robert: No. I can't play. I have no notion of it.

Steve: Do you want me to show you?

Robert: You play?

Steve: Not well. Just basic chords. But I could show you what I know.

Robert: All right.

(Robert holds out the guitar and the piece of paper. Steve takes them both. He puts the paper on the bed and has a look.)

Steve: Ok. That's an A. *(He strums it.)* It's in tune. Tiny little thing. It holds its tune well. Then its C, E minor and A again. G, A and D.

(Steve plays out the chords and reveals the tune.)

Steve: It's good. Who wrote it?

Robert: He did.

Steve: Wow. That's damn good. How old was he?

Robert: Six.

Steve: Clever kid. Although I imagine this needs to be plucked… you know picked… I can't do that. I can only strum it.

(Steve plays it again, feeling it out. This can be improvised by the actor as Steve works out the tune.)

(Robert has suddenly become very somber.)

Steve: You okay there Rob?

Robert: Yeah.

Steve: You sure?

Robert: I never heard his voice.

Steve: What do you mean?

Robert: I never heard his voice. When I hit him, he didn't cry out. You know? I heard his mother screaming. I heard my tires screech. I never heard his voice.

Steve: Maybe that's a good thing. Means he was out straight away.

Robert: I never heard him speak.

(Pause.)

Robert: That guitar. That tune. It's like. It's like his voice. It's all the voice he has.

(Pause. Robert has become emotional, but swallows it down.)

Steve: I know. Do you want to talk to somebody?

Robert: I am talking to somebody.

Steve: Sure.

(Pause.)

Robert: I sometimes wonder. At night mostly. I wonder what he would have done... you know. With his life. Maybe he would have been a pop star. Next Ed Sheerin or something like that.

Steve: I fucking hope not. *(They laugh.)* The next... Hey that was it!

Robert: What?

Steve: Partly truth partly fiction. A walking contradiction. That was Kris Kristofferson.

Robert: Yeah right. The Pilgrim, right?

Steve: Yes.

Robert: Maybe the next Kris Kristofferson.

Steve: Maybe.

(Pause.)

Robert: Maybe he would have worked in a corner store all his life, had a couple of kids and died of booze at sixty-six.

Steve: Maybe. No one'll ever know.

Robert: Maybe he would have cured cancer.

Steve: Could have done something and ended up in this place.

(Pause.)

Steve: He's gone Robert. That's what death is. You can imagine all you want. But… There's nothing to imagine.
    You know something?

Robert: What?

Steve: You've been here nearly two weeks and you've never said his name.

Robert: Really?

Steve: Really.

(Pause.)

Steve: Say his name.

(Pause.)

Robert: Liam. Liam Ramsay.

Steve: Mate, I'm no shrink. You know that. But I think dwelling on what he might have become isn't probably the healthiest thing to do to yourself.

Robert: I can't help it.

Steve: I know. I'm just thinking… His Mum. Is that Maggie?

Robert: Yes.

Steve: You say her name in your sleep a lot. She's probably doing that to herself. She's thinking about what might have been. What grades he would have got in school, his first date, his college graduation. All that. And it can't be good. Because it's just imaginings. You know? It's imaginings that hurt. We can all imagine where we might be if we turned right instead of turning left at some point. There are a thousand roads we'll never travel. There's only the one we're on. And we make our choices and take our turns and we just end up either where we are... or dead. You ended up here. I ended up here. Liam ended up dead. Maggie? She ended up where she ended up too. And she has to work out how to step on now.

Robert: There's a choice to end the journey.

Steve: Don't talk like that, man. They'll take your guitar off you.

Robert: His guitar.

Steve: His guitar.

(Pause.)

Steve: Rob. There's going to be long, long, lonely days in this place for you now. Trust me, I know all about them. You're going to have to find a way to think through these imaginings. Think around them. Or shut them down completely if you can. Because, my friend, they will drive you crazy. You took a turn when you took a turn. That's it now. There's going to be four years in here for it. That's all there is to it. Then there's a new turn to take. Try to think of that day. What are you going to do then? Try to put your head there. If you can.

(Enter Maggie. She has two more toys. She stands and stares at Robert. He looks up at her, lies on his bed and turns away with a groan.)

48

Scene 7

Night.
Robert sits on the floor.
A couple more toys again are on his bed. Eight or more now.
Maggie is in Robert's bed.

Steve: You should try to sleep.

Robert: I can't.

Steve: All right. Well do you mind if I do? I'm pretty wrecked.

(Pause.)

Steve: Okay. I'm off to bed. Good night.

(Steve climbs into bed and pulls the covers over himself. Silence for a time.)

Steve: Good night.

(Silence.)

Steve: Robert, look it would make me feel an awful lot better if you got into bed. I'm worried about you.

(Silence.)

Steve: Do you want me to call a guard?

Robert: Would he let me out?

Steve: That's unlikely, given the nature of prison.

Robert: Then what's the point?

Steve: Just get in your bed, man.

Robert: I don't want to.

(Maggie sits up in the bed.)

Maggie: You don't want to? Why? What's wrong with me?

Steve: Why?

Robert: Don't worry about it.

Maggie: Come on in Robert. There's enough room. Well, enough if we snuggle.

Robert: Fucking hell.

Maggie: Or if you lie on top of me.

Robert: Please stop.

Maggie: Help me make a new boy.

Steve: Ok. I'm sorry.

Maggie: Help me make a new boy, Robert. You killed my first one.

Robert: Not you.

Maggie: Not me?

Steve: Not me?

Robert: It's Maggie. She's in my head. She's in my bed.

Steve: Maggie's in your bed?

Robert: She's in the bed. I can't get in the bed while she's in the bed.

50

Maggie: Come to bed, Robert.

Robert: Please stop. You crazy bitch.

Steve: Robert, I'm calling a guard if you don't stop talking like this, man. Do you actually see a woman in your bed? You know most of the guys in this place would love that.

Robert: *(Standing and pointing.)* There. Right there. Can't you see her?

Steve: No. I see a bed.

Robert: Ah Jesus! My head! Go away!

Maggie: You want me to go away? I'll go away. I'll go away when you tell me the truth. I'll go away when you apologise to me.

Robert: I told you the truth Maggie. I told the court the truth.

Maggie: No. No. No. You didn't tell the truth.

Robert: I did!!

Steve: Robert, stop this now. Come on, man.

Robert: Fuck you Maggie. No more!

Steve: Guard!!

Robert: I will not apologise for something I didn't do! I will not apologise for killing your son if I didn't kill him.

Maggie: You killed him!

Robert: He killed himself!

Maggie: You killed him!

Robert: You killed him!

(Pause. Silence.)

Maggie: I knew it. I knew that's what you thought.

Robert: Why couldn't you have kept the gate closed! Why couldn't you have watched him properly. What kind of a mother are you?

(Silence. Maggie slowly walks out. A moment. Suddenly Robert starts to trash his bed, tearing it up, beating it with his fists, with the pillow. He flings the toys around the room. Steve backs away. Subconsciously he grabs his statue of the Virgin and holds it up to Robert like an exorcist with his crucifix. He notices himself doing this and lowers it again, but keeps hold of it in case he should need to defend himself with it. The Guard enters.)

Guard: Be still man. Be still now.

(Robert goes very still.)

Guard: No harm done. It's all good.

Robert: I'm sorry.

Guard: It's all right now.

Robert: Steve, I'm sorry.

Steve: It's all right.

Guard: We're going to take a break, Robert. We might take a night in the infirmary. Get a bit of rest. Let Cartmell get some rest too. What do you think?

Robert: Sure. Of course.

Guard: Would you turn around for me and face the wall? I better cuff you. I know you're grand, Leversedge, but it's what I'm meant to do. All right?

(Robert does so. The Guard cuffs him and begins to lead him out.)

Robert: I'm sorry, Steve.

Steve: Okay man. Okay. Rest.

(Fade as Robert is brought away.)

ACT II

Scene 1

The next day.
Steve alone writes.
Robert is brought in by the Guard.
He carries the guitar.
More toys.

Guard: Door stays open, Cartmell. I'm right outside. Yes?

Steve: *(With a salute.)* Guard.

(The Guard exits. Silence.)

Steve: How are you?

Robert: Medicated.

Steve: I figured. Did you get some sleep?

Robert: Yes. Just woke up an hour ago. They knocked me out cold.

Steve: What did they give you?

Robert: Valium they said. Must have been a truckload of it. Couldn't have been just valium.

Steve: Diazepan. The cure for all ills.

Robert: Sorry I lost it there last night.

Steve: Hey we all do. Especially early on. In one form or another we lose it.

Robert: Did you?

Steve: Shit yes. I was climbing these walls. Screaming out for the guards to let me out. Demanding to see the warden. My cell mate punched me in the eye. Knocked me out. Didn't need any Valium.

Robert: What did you do?

Steve: Do?

Robert: Yeah. Come on. I want to know what got you seven years in here.

(Pause.)

Steve: I don't like talking about it.

Robert: I know. I'm asking. Might take my mind off things a bit. If you don't mind sharing.

(Pause.)

Steve: All right. For your entertainment I will tell you what I did. But I will also mime as I narrate. Is that all right with you?

Robert: Whatever works.

Steve: All right. Here goes.

(Steve mimes the actions of his story as a kind of odd interpretive dance. This is at the discretion of the director and actor and may involve reflections of the exercises Steve does in Act I or possibly involve the use of the toys.)

Steve: Once there was an importer called Steve. He imported many goods from far away lands and sold them at a profit in Dublin through a variety of outlets and markets. These goods ranged from T-Shirts to Tomatoes, sombrero's to sex toys. Most of the imports came from Eastern Europe, North Africa, South America and Asia. Very cheap, easy to sell. Times were good for a while for Steve and he took out a large mortgage from a very unscrupulous bank on a one hundred and ten percent loan. One day new laws were brought in that raised the taxes and excise on all the products Steve was importing. Things were not so good. Profits were down. Overheads harder to cover. Overdrafts were necessary.

Then the government fucked the country up the arse with a thing called a recession and nobody wanted to buy Steve's exotic goods any more. They had no money. They were like Steve. Every penny went towards trying to keep the mortgage paid and the roof over the head. But Steve went into arrears and the unscrupulous, villainous bank demanded his apartment back unless Steve made a payment.

So one day, Steve was on the docks taking a delivery. He had twelve boxes of pineapples, amongst other things coming in that day. And you see, Robert my dear friend, Steve was screwed and was going to lose his apartment, so he did something to put a little extra money in his pocket that day.

He switched the labels.

Robert: He switched the labels? You switched the labels?

Steve: He switched the labels.

You see, dear listener, for some bizarre reason that only some beauracrat behind a desk could ever possibly explain, the taxes needing to be paid on pineapples were much, much higher than tomatoes. So Steve tore off the pineapple labels that were on those boxes of pineapples and he replaced them with tomato labels.

On the way through customs and excise, where the tarrifs were to be paid, random checks were known but rare. But not rare enough. A grey box cutter handled by a grey-uniformed officer sliced those tomato labeled boxes open and in those boxes were pineapples.

Steve was nicked.

(Pause.)

Robert: Seven fucking years?

Steve: Seven years.

(Pause.)

Robert: Seven fucking years?

(Pause.)

Robert: A priest rapes a little girl and gets…

Steve: I know.

Robert: I…

Steve: A kid runs out in front of your car.

Robert: All right.

(Pause.)

Robert: Seven fucking years?

Steve: The law is an ass.

Robert: I don't believe you.

Steve: That's why I don't like to talk about it. It's unbelievable. Nobody ever really believes it.

Robert: That's all you did? Switched labels to avoid a few bob in excise duty.

Steve: Yup.

Robert: Bullshit. Who did you stab?

Steve: Look Rob. I broke the law. I admit it. I did it. Look, the fact is, if they hadn't busted me that day, I was heading to the wall anyway. Within six months I was going to be living on the streets. I was a gay man living alone. I didn't have a lot of friends and certainly no rich ones. My parents are dead. Who was I going to go to? Who was going to catch me when I fell?

At least in here it's warm, I have a roof over my head, I have a bed, three square meals a day, and I have the convivial company of the Virgin Mary and whatever hardened crook ends up in that bed there.

The taxpayer saved me from the streets.

And I have simplicity. I'm not built for the world outside here, Rob. I'm like a scared mouse out there. In here I have my routine. I have my bed.

Robert: You don't belong in here. Nobody belongs in here.

Steve: I do. I don't ever want to leave. Where will I go? What will I do?

Robert: But seven years?

Steve: If the people who run this country think switching labels on boxes deserves more prison time than the rape of children, there's nothing I can do about that. It just shows you their priorities. Money in their coffers first, the well-being of their children a distant last.

So much for aiming for a world made for children, right Rob? What did you say? Playful? Safe? Free? Something like that?

This world is lost.

(Pause.)

Robert: What about John? Couldn't he have helped you out?

Steve: He has a family. He lost his job around that time too. And all the shit with his daughter and the courts had drained him. He met me in a bar one night. He was so confused and fucked up at the time, he offered to pay me for sex. I let him. Which was a shit thing to do because I thought we were… you know… getting along. Which we were. But when he offered to pay me… I don't know I got kind of offended or something. It's hard to say what happened there. I felt sorry for him too. I don't know.

(Pause.)

Steve: In fact I have no fucking idea why I'm telling you all this. Have I distracted you enough from your hallucinations of Maggie yet?

Robert: Yes. Well she's not around. So it's you or the meds or something.

Steve: I swear to God. Once my mouth opens, it's like diarrhea. I'm sorry.

Robert: Sorry for what? You're life is fascinating to this boring accountant.

Steve: She's not under the bed is she?

Robert: I'll check. (He does.) Nope.

Steve: That's good.

Robert: Thank you.

Steve: That's okay.

Robert: Really. I needed that. You're a friend.

Steve: Well we might as well be friends. We have a long time to chat.

(Pause.)

Robert: Can I ask you something personal?

Steve: More personal?

Robert: Sort of.

Steve: Go on, so. In for a penny…

Robert: How did you know you were gay?

Steve: That's a dumb question.

Robert: Is it? I don't think it is.

Steve: I just knew. When I was about twelve I guess. I realized I liked boys better than girls. I fanticised about boys instead of girls.

Robert: Okay. I just wondered. Because I never had an inkling of anything like that. You know? I just wondered how it happens.

Steve: You know, I have a theory.

Robert: What's your theory?

Steve: I have a theory that most straight people are homophobic.

Robert: That's a dumb theory.

Steve: Really? So have you fanticised about having sex with a man?

Robert: No. Because I'm straight.

Steve: Go on and fanticise about it.

Robert: If you're trying to turn me, it's not going to happen Steve.

Steve: I'm not trying to turn you. I'm just saying that I think you're homophobic.

Robert: I'm not afraid of you Steve. You can be sure of that.

Steve: Then fantasize about being with a man. Go on. Think about it.

Robert: I don't want to. Why would I. I like women.

Steve: I'll tell you why you don't. Because you're afraid. You're afraid that if you really let yourself fantasize about sex with a man, you might feel that familiar feeling of actual arousal. Even just a moment of it. And that terrifies you. As such, even though you are politically correct, even though you would go out on that street and wave that rainbow flag with all your fag and dyke mates, deep down you're actually, by definition, homophobic... that is, afraid not of gays as such, but afraid of being gay. Afraid of the possibility that arousal might happen if you think about the same sex act too much.

Robert: You're on the wrong track Steve. Seriously.

Steve: Does the idea of two women turn you on?

Robert: I don't think I want to answer these questions.

Steve: Why? Are you afraid?

Robert: No. Sure. The idea of two women together is... all right.

Steve: So think about two men being together in the same way...

Robert: No.

Steve: Why not? Because you're afraid it might turn you on.

Robert: It won't turn me on!

Steve: But how do you know unless you give it time in your mind?

(Pause.)

Robert: Stop fucking with my head.

Steve: We're all children just trying to find out who we are. We choose what rabbit holes we go down. That's all it is. That's all I think it is anyway.

Scene 2

A time Lapse.
A few days.
Lots of toys. On the bed, on the floor on Robert's side of the cell.
He can't move for kicking them.
The sounds of the guitar roughly playing the chords of The River.
Lights come up.

Steve: That's coming along.

Robert: It's ok. Clunky. I can get the chords. It's changing from one to the other in time that's hard.

Steve: I know. There's a little jump the second time you play that D.

Robert: What? Where?

Steve: I'll show you.

(Steve takes the guitar and shows Robert the quick pre-time jump on the second D.)

Steve: Get it?

Robert: That's too quick. I'll never get that.

Steve: How do you get to Carnegie Hall Robert?

Robert: I know. I know.

(He tries and fails. His fingers hurt. He stops.)

Robert: I'll get it. Just not today.

(Pause.)

Steve: How's the meds?

Robert: Good. They're going to take me off the Luvox Monday. My head's swimming from it.

Steve: Any voices?

Robert: No voices.

Steve: Can I ask you something?

Robert: Sure.

Steve: What was she actually saying to you?

Robert: Maggie?

Steve: Yes.

Robert: Crazy stuff. She was blaming herself. Blaming Liam. Wanting me to blame myself so she wouldn't have to blame herself and Liam. She wanted me to tell the truth. She kept saying "tell the truth". But I did tell the truth. I stood up in court and I told the truth. She wanted an apology. See, if I apologise it means an admission of guilt, which means I'm completely culpable. There's no responsibility on her or her son for what happened. That's what she wants. She just wants to feel free of it by dumping it all on me.

Steve: Then why don't you?

Robert: What?

Steve: Just take the responsibility. Let the poor woman off the hook. Just admit you were slow on the brake because of the drink. Then she can leave herself alone. She must be tearing herself to pieces. Think of it from her perspective. She's lost her son. Her son. Now we don't have kids so we don't know what that's like but think about that for a second. She carried that boy in her womb for nine months and then bore him into the world, then devoted her life to him for six years. Put yourself in her shoes.

Not only did she lose her son, the court decided that the fault wasn't all yours but mitigated, meaning it was partly her fault for not watching him, and partly his own fault for tearing out into the road. The court basically said to her that she killed her own child.

You got four years. She got life, Rob. She's never going to forgive herself. You've forgiven yourself because you've decided you did nothing wrong by drinking those pints. She's in limbo.

Robert: Hold the fucking phone, Steve.
Are you suggesting that I lie?

Steve: Lie?

Robert: Yeah. Are you suggesting that I tell Maggie... what... that I had seven pints? That I lost concentration? That I drifted off? That I could have stopped if I hadn't had those drinks? Do you have any idea how long I'd be sitting in here if the court found that was the truth?

Steve: Probably seven years like me.

Robert: But that's not what happened. Why would I invent something false? What possible result could that have? I'll tell you what the result of that would be. I'd be in here for a shit load longer than four years, for something that's untrue, all to help a woman alleviate her own conscience *(suddenly he screams these next words out)* FOR LEAVING HER FUCKING GATE OPEN AND NOT WATCHING HER FUCKING KID!

(Long silence.)

Steve: You want to hear another Steve story?

Robert: No.

Steve: Well I'll tell you anyway. Door's open if you want to leave.
When Steve was a little tike, just ten years old, he was riding a BMX bike with his neighbours. His parents didn't let him have a bike

of his own. He prayed every year for a bike from Santa and Santa never brought him one. The cunt. Steve was never really sure if Santa was a cunt, or just didn't exist and his parents were cunts, or that his parents were afraid he'd get hurt on a bike, or that his parents were just poor and couldn't afford a bike for him. A bike was expensive back then.

He was never really sure, but because his parents didn't like to talk about it, he figured it was a money thing. But his neighbours had bikes. Two boys lived next door and for some reason they had four bikes, as if each of those boys had two arses.

When his parents weren't looking, the boys next door would let Steve ride one of their bikes. Steve would fly around the houses, in and out of back yards and gardens, across roads and back again. It was his favourite thing in the whole world to do. It made him feel free as a bird, Robert. But too free, because he had never had a bike of his own and therefore had never been taught about how to use it and the rules of the road. Steve had no road sense whatsoever. He didn't know the rules. He didn't know there even WERE rules.

And then one day, yes you guessed it my intrepid listener, Steve rode straight out in front of a big, banana coloured car and it cleaned him up good an proper.

What happened exactly was this. There was a little jump off a gutter that Steve would love to shoot over. He would get airborne on it. And it would bring him down in the middle of the road. He would always look to his right to see if any cars were coming, but there rarely would be because the road was a dead end. On this day, Steve took a look, saw the yellow car way down the end of the road and knew he had plenty of time to ride, jump and clear the road long before the car was near him. But he heard the car rev. It was speeding up. The driver was in a hurry. Did he still have enough time? In his head, he thought yes, it's way down the end of the road. Tons of time. And besides that he's committed to the jump and had worked up the pace he needed for the feat.

He hit the jump, got airborne and came down right in the middle of the road as he had planned, but the back tire slid off the rim of the wheel. The rim ground into the tarmac and the bike stopped dead. Right in the middle of the road.

The banana car had worked up a good pace, and although the driver, a middle aged woman who was selling door to door cosmetics, slammed on her brakes, it was too late for the stranded Steve who was still, like a deer in the headlights, right in the middle of that road.

Bang. Steve was knocked off the bike and rolled up the road like a crash test dummie. Somehow he didn't break any bones, but he lost most of the skin off his knees and arms. His helmetless head too was somehow spared. Other than a nauseating dose of shock and lot of scabs, Steve had a lucky escape.

The bike, however, wasn't so lucky. Although Steve was knocked clear, the big yellow beast of a car rolled over the bike and crunched it beneath, stopping on top of it.

Steve didn't give a fuck about his injuries. With blood pouring off his limbs, he got up and started to pull his bike out from under the front of the car. He could hear his mother screaming and running towards him. But when he looked down at the bike, mangled and mashed and destroyed, Steve knew he was in some seriously deep shit.

Number 1. It wasn't his bike. Fuck!

Number 2. His father, a disciplinarian to put it mildly, would have to pay for the bike... when he couldn't afford a bike for his own son. Fuck!

And Number 3. If there was any chance whatsoever that his parents were ever going to get him a bike of his own, it was now shot to shit. For good. Forever.... Fuck.

(Pause.)

Robert: That's it? Good story.

Steve: That's not it. I'm going to abandon 3rd person now if you don't mind.

Robert, here's the thing. It wasn't until I was in this cell, in my first year here, and had all the time in the world to think about all the memories of my childhood and youth and all the things I'd done and seen and experienced, that I took the time to be honest with myself about that day over twenty years ago.

Robert: Honest?

Steve: Yes. Honest. In that moment I was instantly terrified. Terrified of what my neighbours would do, what my father would do, how my mother would react by refusing ever to get me a bike.

In that moment I invented a whole scenario of excuses. I saw the car down the bottom of the road. No I didn't. I never even looked. But I invented that image and burned it onto my brain as if it was real. I heard it rev its engine. No I didn't. Invented. But I could hear that sound. The tire came off the rim when I came down on the road. Nope. All bullshit. I needed to be able to tell my neighbours and my parents that it wasn't all my fault, that I wasn't just completely irresponsible and stupid. That I didn't ruin the bike. That I deserved a bike of my own because this wasn't all my fault.

But Robert, I rode out from behind my house that day with one thing on my mind, getting up as much pace as possible so I could get enough air to break my own personal best distance for that jump.

I was a ten year old kid who made a mistake. And that poor woman shook like a leaf and cried in front of me that day and I glared at her like it was her fault. And it wasn't. It was mine.

Now here's my point. I drummed that story into my head so deeply that it became my memory. Do you understand what I'm saying? I invented my memory of that day. I told it to myself over and over as I lay in bed in shock that afternoon, shaking, a sick bowl by my side, my mother washing the dirt and tiny stones out of my wounds, waiting in fear for my father to come home from work. I told my mother that story, then I told him that story and then I told everyone else and then I told myself over and over and over for years and years and years.

And when I was finally able, only two years ago to admit that I was a ten year old kid who fucked up? God it was such a relief. It was so liberating to actually admit the real truth to myself. It didn't matter what my parents or my neighbours thought. It didn't even matter what that woman who was driving that banana thought. If there was any fault in any of them at all, it was that they brought such fear and pressure to bear on a little boy that he thought he needed to invent an intricate lie in an instant in order to protect himself from the terrible repercussions he so feared.

But we do, Robert. We can and we do. We invent intricate lies in an instant. (Steve snaps his fingers.) Just like that.

Two years ago that ten year old kid called Steve was finally able to forgive himself for making a mistake. He deserved that. And he was able to leave that road for the first time. He was only a boy. And everybody can fuck up, Robert. Everybody.

(Pause.)

Robert: How do you know?

Steve: Know what?

Robert: If the sight of the car down the road, the rev of its engine, all of it, seemed so real, how do you know you made it up?

Steve: Because no matter how deep you bury the truth, it's always there somewhere. And if you're quiet for long enough, you can hear it whisper, then speak. We can invent intricate lies in an instant. It takes time to see through them to the simple truth.

Robert: What are you saying? That I've invented what happened that day I hit Liam? That I've told the court a huge lie that I don't even know is a lie?

Steve: I'm not saying that. What I'm saying is, don't carry it around for twenty years if you have. The Judge made a sentence for you. Four years. Better to serve seven with the truth. Better to serve seven and be free in yourself.

Robert: And be stuck in here for seven years like you? Fuck that.
    Besides I've told the truth. My conscience is clear. I've got nothing to hide.

Steve: Rob, you're a good guy. You know a little boy is dead. You know how much pain Maggie is in. What you've probably forgotten; and the Judge and the court and everyone else has forgotten this too, I bet; is that you went through a trauma here too. In the same way I went through a trauma when I was hit by that car when I was ten. I went into shock. Shock is a medical thing. A clinical, real thing with symptoms and side effects. Your brain went into shock and probably into damage control.

Look, all I'm saying is that maybe, in all the chaos and the mayhem and the pressure of the trial and being sentenced to prison for four years and your whole life as you knew it being snuffed out... maybe your brain has been in shock ever since. You saw a dead child on the road in front of your car. I've never seen a dead child, let alone one I hit with my car. Is it not conceivable that your brain went into a state of shock and damage control and perhaps invented a scenario of what happened that could protect you? At least to some degree?

(Pause.)

Robert: The truth is a complex thing.

Steve: Not really.

Robert: Steve, the truth is rarely pure and never simple.

Steve: You're wrong there, Rob. It's always pure and always simple. Oscar Wilde wrote comedies about delusional people. Think before you quote. Now I need to take a dump so would you mind stepping out?

(Robert looks at him a moment. And fade.)

Scene 3

Night. Robert and Steve are in their beds asleep. Silence. Maggie enters in the blue darkness and stands. Robert senses her presence. He turns to her and slowly sits up. Maggie's arms are by her sides. Slowly she turns her hands palm-out to Robert. A reflection of Steve's Virgin Mary statue. A long moment.

Robert: *(whispering)*
    I'm sorry.

Maggie: I know.

(Robert goes to her and kneels at her feet. He embraces her and places his head against her womb. She enfolds him in her arms.)

Maggie: Thank you.

(Steve wakes and goes to Robert as he kneels on the floor. Maggie steps away and exits.)

Steve: Rob?

(Silence.)

Steve: Come on Rob. Let's get you back to bed.

(Robert "wakes" but barely. His face is wet with tears. Disoriented he makes his way back to his feet, then to his bed with Steve's help. Steve lays him down. Covers him with the blanket.)

Scene 4

Robert plays the guitar. A clunky, yet less clunky version of The River. Steve writes. Robert stops playing.

Robert: You want to hear a Robert story?

(Steve stops writing and turns to Robert.)

Robert: Once there was a man called Robert who turned thirty years old and went for lunch in a pub with his mates. They kept buying him pints because it was his birthday and he kept drinking them. He figured he'd had a big meal he was a big enough lad, so a few pints wouldn't hurt. He couldn't leave his car where it was because it would get clamped, so after three pints he decided to drive home.

He was driving up a familiar hill and at the top, on the left was a house. It had a low, black gate. He could see from a long distance that the gate was open. He noticed it. He slowed down a little as he came up the rise because at the top of the hill the road dipped down suddenly and he didn't like the feeling of butterflies in his belly. Never did. Even as a child.

Just as he came near to the house a small boy ran out into the road. Robert saw the boy and hit the brakes immediately, but it was too late. The bumper hit the boy and the boy was thrown backwards, hitting his head on the hard pavement and breaking his back.

He died right there on the road. There was nothing Robert could do. There was nothing Robert could have done.

Steve: That's an interesting story.

Robert: Thanks.

Steve: Do you want to tell me another one?

(Pause.)

Robert: Once there was a man called Robert who went to lunch with his mates on his thirtieth birthday. He drove into town that day, figuring he'd have a meal and maybe a pint or two over a good few hours and he'd be grand to drive. But his mates kept buying him pints, naturally, and Robert kept drinking them. And after a while he was having such a good time, he decided to leave his car where it was and just cop the fine and the clamp. It was his birthday after all.

He drank six, maybe seven pints.

He was well pissed when the party started to break up around 4pm. He decided to risk it and drive the dam car home anyway. Why cop a clamping? He felt fine. He felt more than fine. He felt super-confident. He felt great. He was the birthday boy!

Just in case, he avoided the main roads where the cops might have breath tests set up on a Saturday afternoon and he took some residential streets home.

He was on his way up a straight hill. He knew it well. There was a rise at the top. He figured if he put his foot down a bit he could get a bit of a leap at the top; get that butterflies in the belly feeling he loved so much as a kid. So he put his foot down.

Just at the top of the hill he closed his eyes for a brief second to really feel that sensation of those butterflies. And there was a horrible clunk. He hit the brakes. He had no idea what had happened.

A woman was screaming. He got out of the car and a little boy was lying on the road and a lot of blood was coming out of the back of his head.

Robert cried over and over, "he just ran out!" "he just ran out!" "he just ran out".

It was all Robert could say.

He just ran out.

(Silence. After a moment Steve goes to Robert and puts his hand on his shoulder.)

Robert: Can I get a piece of paper and a pencil? I have to write a letter.

Steve: To Maggie?

Robert: No. Not to Maggie.

Steve: To who? What are you going to do?

76

Robert: I'm going to take a turn.

Scene 5

The Late Late Toy Show. A spotlight on a stool on which sits Robert with the guitar. Another spot in which all the soft toys are set.

Robert: Hello.

I know this is unconventional. To have a man you don't know playing a guitar on the Toy Show. I really appreciate you letting me do this.

A year ago a little boy ran out in front of my car. He died that day. His dream was to play his guitar, this guitar on the Late Late Toy Show.

(Pause. Robert clears his throat and starts again.)

Robert: A year ago I killed a boy with my car because I'd been drinking. I made a mistake. I'm serving a four-year prison sentence.

That boy's name was Liam Ramsay. He was six. He wanted to be sitting here with this guitar right now playing it for you. But he's not. He can't. And that's all my fault. My fault. And my fault alone.

I know it's not easy because I'm a man. But if we all together try to imagine a boy sitting where I am, here on this stool, perhaps we can hear his voice through this little guitar.

Because that's all his mother or his father or his friends... or me... can ever have of him again. An imagining of Liam.

He wrote this tune. It's called The River. It's his voice. It's the last sounds of a beautiful boy... who I killed.

(Robert plays The River.)

(Fade.)

End